STRANGE CHILDREN

Strange Children by Dan Brady
First published in 2018 by Publishing Genius Press
Atlanta, GA
www.publishinggenius.com

ISBN: 978-1-945028-12-0

Book design by Adam Robinson
Cover design and drawing by Jarod Roselló

Visit danbrady.org, Tweet @danbrady82

STRANGE CHILDREN
DAN BRADY

Publishing
Genius Press

FIVE YEARS LATER

STROKE DIARY

Even now I see her
touch thumb to forefinger,
thumb to middle finger,
thumb to ring finger,
thumb to little finger.

And again. Three times.

Her hand is where it started.
First reaching for the door knob,

or believing she is reaching,
but falling inches short.

Later, with the baby,
reaching for the blanket,

or believing she is reaching;
her hand does not move.

Her right hand.
Her right leg.

Her right eye.
Her right side.

I call the doctor.
Describe. Ask.

The doctor
and my wife

speak in stereo:
Call 911.

The feeling
and the fear

come
and go.

When the seizure
starts
I hold
her down.

Half of her
constricts.

She slams
her wrist
into
her chest,
hard.

After, her greatest desire
is to pull the nasal trumpet

from her face. The nurse asks me
to calm her. Tell her it's okay,

leave the trumpet
in its place.

The ICU is cold
and dark in the evening.

An MRI shows
a clot on her brain.

The doctor points
to the back of her neck,

along her hairline,
behind her ear. Here.

Ventilators bellow
slow air.

She's the youngest
person in the stroke unit

by forty years.
A nurse watches

through a window
in the wall.

Fear, like an aneurysm, bleeds,
uncontainable but by skull.

Thumb, forefinger.
Thumb, middle finger.
Thumb, ring finger.
Thumb, little finger.
Repeat.

Here is where we learn
our mantra.

The treatment is less than exact.
A series of guesses to find the right levels.

Too much and the clot will bleed—
            hemorrhage—
    death.

Too little and the clot will grow—
            brain damage—
    death.

Death walks the halls
checking through windows

in walls, switching off machines,
silencing alarms as if they were nothing.

Death comes in the room as an observer,
just as I am.

Our life together,
like a great whale

breaching, or rather
as fast as a fish

picks a single fly
from the river water.

The doctor says
she will be fine.

Thumb, forefinger.
Thumb, middle finger.
Thumb, ring finger.
Thumb, little finger.
Repeat.

At home, I never leave
her alone. I watch

as I know she's watching,
as I know he's watching.

In the car:

Thumb, forefinger.
Thumb, middle finger.
Thumb, ring finger.
Thumb, little finger.
Repeat.

On the couch:

Thumb, forefinger.
Thumb, middle finger.
Thumb, ring finger.
Thumb, little finger.
Repeat.

Before the mirror:

Thumb, forefinger.
Thumb, middle finger.
Thumb, ring finger.
Thumb, little finger.
Repeat.

The stroke never ends for us.
Fear, the longest lasting side effect.

A ghost symptom.
And so.

Thumb, forefinger.
Thumb, middle finger.
Thumb, ring finger.
Thumb, little finger.
Repeat.

Thumb, forefinger.
Thumb, middle finger.
Thumb, ring finger.
Thumb, little finger.
Repeat.

Thumb, forefinger.
Thumb, middle finger.
Thumb, ring finger.
Thumb, little finger.
Repeat.

At least three times.

THERE IS AN ENEMY IN LOVE

There is an enemy in Love,
you know what I mean?

The fear of it. It
comes on like a wave.

To be understood
could be a terrible thing.

There is death in Love,
you know what I mean?

The shame of it all
laid bare.

To see me break like a wave
and the welling undertow.

Better to be safe. Better to be
separate and alone

because then I could sleep at night.
You know what I mean?

Without anyone ever
pressing against me.

Without breath, nearly inaudible,
reminding me that death is in the room.

Yes, there is an enemy in Love
and I will not face it

because I am afraid of what I am.
You know what I mean?

A NEWBORN FACT

After the stroke, it was the cardiologist
who told us, not the neurologist
or even the OB GYN, though
we found out they all agreed.
"When a woman gets pregnant
her blood naturally thickens.
Clots are always a risk—
usually in the legs or arms—
but in you
the clot formed on your brain.
Given the risk of recurrence,
you shouldn't get pregnant again."
And there it was. A new fact
born into our lives.

We went home with our newborn
and our newborn fact
and let our imagined futures
dissolve like blood clots
soaking in a stream of Heparin,
carried away in pieces,
like the tingling fade
of a trans ischemic attack,

like salt in a wound.

His name was Dr. Disby—
chest hair peaking over his collar,
a wide gap between his front teeth.
Maybe they chose him because,
more than anything, this was a matter
of the heart. Har har. No, it was because
most of his patients have cancer.
He is comfortable telling people
their lives will be much different
than what they'd wanted.
He knows the way blood moves
through a body, how it changes,
bringing life to limbs and organs,
while dying and replenishing along the way.

And so a subtle re-negotiation
of all our thoughts began, adjusting all our plans,
mourning the loss of what we never had
but dreamt of—not allowed to dream
of that life any longer. We would create
new dreams for ourselves. Simpler dreams—
or more daring ones. This new little fact
had arrived in our lives and now
he was ours to raise up however we saw fit.

WHERE TO BEGIN

for Reid

The way you explore this space
is the way life happens.

Walk it out. Feel around.
You'll find that on occasion

your senses betray you
and everything becomes light.

Other times a crushing weight
compresses you to your tiniest form.

It is our hope you will be moved easily,
that you will be more air than earth,

that you will find pleasures yet undiscovered
and that the darkness lasts only briefly.

We cannot promise this,
only assure you of our intentions.

There are many experiments
and most of them die.

Those that succeed
find advantage in their environment.

They see what no one else sees.
Out of love, they create new possibilities.

LIGHT YEAR

To measure your loss
you must account
for time and distance.
You'll find as time
increases, distance
remains unchanged.
Speed will increase,
as loss makes you lighter.

It's not mathematical
exactly. It's physical.
The light year measures
distance in a vacuum—
how fast we can flee
the suck and stillness
of absence.

PROGRESS

Hey, I got your text
about not wanting
to have this
conversation.
I totally understand.
It's uncomfortable
for me too.
I hope we can
pick it up again
some other time.
I do think
it's important.
We can change
our behaviors,
the way we treat
each other,
our attitudes.
I believe that.
So thanks.

WHAT HAPPENS WHEN IT STOPS

This tree will never grow.

This pot will never boil.

This book will never be read.

This painting will never be seen.

This engine will never start.

This plum will never be eaten.

This bee will never dance.

This guitar will never play.

This drum will never beat.

This light will never shine.

This door will never open.

This screw will never turn.

This bread will never rise.

This rain will never fall.

This wave will never roll.

This tooth will never bite.

This mountain will never stay.

This mind will never think.

This heart will never break.

This friend will never leave.

This eye will never cry.

This hand will never reach.

This center will never hold.

This flower will never smell.

This screen will never show.

This wheel will never turn.

This wait will never end.

This wind will never blow.

But love, what happens

to this love?

FIVE YEARS LATER

ON GRIEF AND GRATEFULNESS

In the new baby's room where there is no baby yet
we wait in anguish and expectation.
We've been through this before
and know that a phone call
isn't a sure thing—and even if it is,
the work begins with life.

When you adopt, you fill out
a "child desired" form
to articulate how comfortable you are
being uncomfortable. Race, genetics,
drugs, disease, mental health,
gender, religion, openness.
It's all uncomfortable.
You need to know
how much you can handle.
You need to know
how weak you can be.

I worry.
I worry
about questions
from strangers.
Will I have
the right answers?
Right for me,
right for them,
but most of all,
right for my child.
Right.

While we wait I imagine hundreds of children
none of whom are mine, all of whom are mine.
And I wish for a world for any child,
any adult, anyone. This baby is coming
from where and when I don't know, and
it will be my responsibility and I will take it up
and take up the world and grow them together
like a peacemaker and a peace-making tyrant.

It occurs to me: This is what Jesus means by
sons, daughters, brothers, sisters.
This is the dream of literature, isn't it?
To experience another possible life
and understand its struggles. But
this is not faith or fiction. This is life.
My life. My children's lives.
Human lives lived together.

What you see is a beauty rooted in tragedy.
Families torn apart and reassembled.
It is often easiest to see the best
of humanity only after catastrophe.
What goodness there is now does not erase the pain of then.
Once an event occurs it continues forever.

My daughter
was three years old
and had been living
with her mother.
My son
had a twenty
percent chance
of developing
cystic fibrosis.
My other daughter
was conceived
through incest.
My other son's mother
decided to parent
in her hospital bed.
My other son
tasted liquor
in the womb.
The twins were
my only set of twins.

I have lived a thousand lives
with these children and the grief
and joy of each one is a blessing to me.
Wherever they are and whatever
becomes of them, I thank them.
And I thank them
and I thank them
and I thank them
and I wait.

BREAK IT DOWN

In the summer we receive more guests
and I break down the crib in the baby's room
as the baby has not come yet and this feels
like betrayal, like giving up.
But it's practicality. With an extra bed in the house,
Tessa won't have to sleep on the pullout
that she hates each time she visits. But still
it feels wrong, as if it symbolizes some failure
of faith on my part. When I asked Christina
if we should put the crib away, she paused
for a long moment, then said *yes*.
I have to remind myself that symbolism
is just something poets invented to get jobs
at universities. I'm just breaking down
one bed for another. Nothing more. The baby
will be here soon and then I'll break down
this bed for the crib with no second thoughts.

THE OLDEST WORDS,
THE OLDEST WOUNDS

Birth Parents Meeting

To hear
a mother's hand
put to the fire's flow,
pulled back
black as bark.

Who is
this old man?
Spit,
worms,
and ashes.

LULLABY FOR THE WAITING

When in space asleep
there is no up or down.

Your breath floats above you,
a mask of carbon dioxide.

The mind forgets
its weightlessness

when waking—
a terror every time—

but the sun rises
every ninety minutes

and it is always
a new day.

Sleep tight,
little astronauts.

PLEXUS

after Gabriel Dawe

Sea glass
threadbare

time's drift
slow drip

kite string
don't care

she knows
I'm there

rainbow
wave break

light show
can't fake

yarn ball
color wheel

is this
how it feels

coming
coming

coming
coming

A FAILURE

Birth Mother Meeting

He saw
the woman
weeping
and prayed
for her
but not
with her.

THE MORNING IS A SEA

The morning is a sea
and the whole world
sloshes about
with possibility.
Why are so many things
shaped like waves?
A conductor's wand
as it moves through the air.
The spiral curls of your hair.
The in and out of breaths.
The crush of a violent death.
Because a wave never truly stops.
It is reabsorbed, reshaped.
Continues again.
There is no shame in failure
because there is no end.
Try again. On our saddest days,
we can still seek and we
can still find. We are seekers
and finders, all of us, sloshing
about. It helps not to have
a stated goal. A wave
always finds the shore
eventually, even if
just for a moment.
Today could be the day.

The sun is bright upon
the waves. So bright
I can hardly see
if we're moving toward
each other or drifting
farther apart.
It doesn't matter really.
When night comes
we won't be able to see
each other anyway
but we'll feel like we're together
as we look up at the darkening sky,
into that distant past,
and find ourselves
part of the same ocean,
the same pull and swell,
and that will be enough
until morning comes again.

DOES JESUS SLEEP

Does Jesus sleep
in his waiting for me?

In the Bible, God
remembers
and takes pity.

We too need
reminders—rituals

to not forget those
commandments.

Do this in memory
of me, He said,
and we do.

Does God have His rituals?

When this quasar pulses
I will remember you, Jane Anne.

When this blade of grass wavers,
I remember you, Hans Peter.

When this grain of sand
is returned to the sea,
I will think of you, Frank.

In the beginning
was the Word,
the promise.

But promises
can be forgotten
without being broken.

The ritual of delay
and fulfillment.

QUESTIONS OF HISTORY

Birth Mother Meeting

Questions
of history
rarely concern
the past.
You can never know
how strong
you'll need to be.
How much courage
is enough.
It takes
a lifetime
to know
another.
Babies grab
any finger.

AN OPENING

Birth Parents Meeting

A combination
lock of wounds
such as this
requires
careful listening,
subtle shifts,
lest we be
sealed off
from each other
forever.

SUMMER

It was the summer
your mom broke her back,
face, and arm.
It was the summer
the family of five
moved into our basement.
It was the summer
my parents fled
to Texas.
It was the summer
you finally got the raise
you deserved two years ago.
It was the summer
spent prepping
for kindergarten.
It was the summer
when we tried to be
better people
mostly through
flower delivery services.
It was the summer
we wanted to master
French Onion Soup.
It was the summer

the baby's adoption
came through
and our house was
at once full and quiet,
joyful and grieving,
dark and bright.
It was the summer
that changed our lives
from what we had been
and what we were becoming
to what we are
and are becoming now.
After the exterminators
sprayed the backyard,
the mosquitos stayed away
for three weeks straight
and every night
we made a fire pit
and every night
we drank wine
and every night
we went to sleep
exhausted and happy
and ready to wake.

NOTES

A few lines of "Stoke Diary" first appeared on telephone poles, fence posts, and street signs around Baltimore as part of *IsReads*. Thanks to Adam Robinson.

"Stroke Diary" was later published in its entirety in *apt*. Thanks to Carissa Halston and Randolph Pfaff.

"There Is an Enemy in Love" appeared in *Everyday Genius*. Thanks to Adam Robinson.

"What Happens When It Stops" owes a debt to Justin Marks.

"A New Born Fact" and "Lullaby for the Waiting" appeared in *Beltway Poetry Quarterly*. Thanks to Kim Roberts and Gowri Koneswaran.

"Questions of History" appeared in *Sink Review*. Thanks to Steven Karl and Dan Magers.

"The Oldest Words, the Oldest Wounds" is comprised of the oldest known words in the English language.

"Plexus" was written for the So & So Reading Series, hosted during CAM Raleigh's exhibition of installations by Gabriel Dawes. Thanks to Chris Tonelli.

ON GRATEFULNESS

When I read these poems I see the people behind them.

Thank you to my parents Dan and Cathy Brady. Thanks to the poets and friends and teachers who provided invaluable feedback on this work: Tony Mancus, Catie Rosemurgy, Mark Cugini, Maureen Thorson, Thea Brown, Carrie Murphy, Rebekah Sankey, Lee Posna, Michael Turner, and Meg Ronan.

Thank you to the whole Barrelhouse crew for their constant support, candor, companionship, and humor: Becky Bernard, Killian Czuba, Erin Fitzgerald, Chris Gonzales, Dave Housley, Mike Ingram, Joe Killiany, Tom McAlister, Susan Muaddi-Darraj, Matt Perez, and Sheila Squillante.

Thank you God and Adam Robinson for making this book possible.

Finally, thank you to my wife Christina. I love you. Thank you for your encouragement, your kindness, your openness, and your strength. Thank you for doing all of this with me.

THE AUTHOR

Dan Brady is the author of two chapbooks, *Cabin Fever / Fossil Record* (Flying Guillotine Press) and *Leroy Sequences* (Horse Less Press). Recent poems have appeared or are forthcoming in *Apt*, *Sink Review*, and *So & So Magazine*. He is the poetry editor of *Barrelhouse* and lives in Arlington, Virginia with his wife and two kids. *Strange Children* is his first full-length poetry collection. Learn more at danbrady.org.

Also visit PublishingGenius.com